FROM TRIENT PRESS

Robert
Balsley

THE
LOSS
OF
INNOCENCE

ROBERT E. BALSLEY, JR

Trient Press

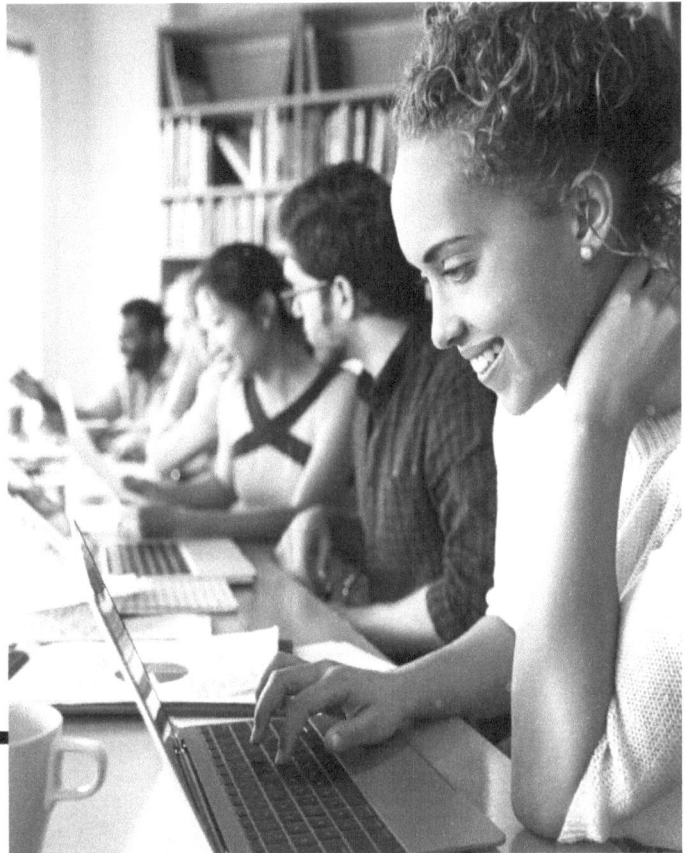

TRIENTREPRENEUR

ISSUE 6

CAPITAL SCHOOL

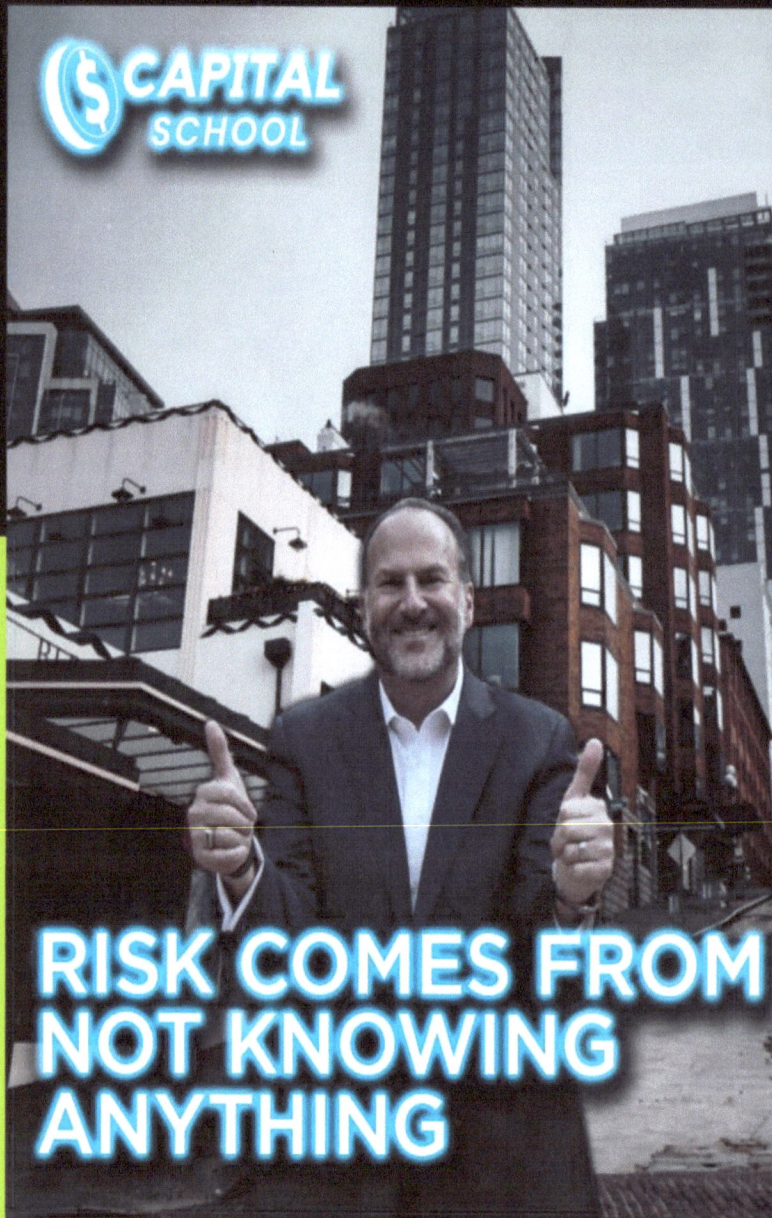

RISK COMES FROM NOT KNOWING ANYTHING

TODAY, CAPITAL SCHOOL IS ONE OF THE FASTEST GROWING COMMUNITIES OF ENTREPRENEURS, BUSINESS OWNERS, CEOS AND OTHERS LEARNING HOW TO ATTRACT, RAISE, AND CLOSE HNW INVESTOR CAPITAL. IT DOESN'T MATTER WHETHER YOU'RE NEW TO RAISING MONEY OR HAVE BEEN DOING IT FOR AWHILE - CAPITAL SCHOOL CAN HELP YOU GET TO THE NEXT LEVEL.

WHAT'S INCLUDED IN CAPITAL SCHOOL:

GET ACCESS TO MY FREE TRAINING
- HOW TO ATTRACT INVESTOR CAPITAL
- FOUR STEP BLUEPRINT TO RAISING CAPITAL
- SECURITIES LAWS | REGULATIONS
- CROWDFUNDING 101
- ACCESSING HNW LISTS
- GETTING INTO FAMILY OFFICES AND B/DS
- PLATFORMS FOR CAPITAL
- LINKS TO FAMILY OFFICE NETWORKS
- PUTTING YOUR "PITCH DECK AND OFFERING MATERIALS TOGETHER"
- AND MORE

SEPTEMBER TIPS

Advice about marketing

- Look for Opportunities to Diversify.
- Embrace Paid Social.
- Focus On Your Existing Content.
- Nurture Brand Advocates.
- Constantly Optimize User Experience.
- Connect Online and Offline Strategies.
- Prioritize Authenticity.
- Create a Memorable Message.

THE 5 BEST WAYS

to Dramatically Increase Productivity

PRL

Being productive at work can be challenging. It can be hard to know where to start managing your time in ways that are conducive to your productivity. No matter who you are, it can be a struggle to understand how to structure your time effectively. No matter who you are or what you do for work, you need to be on point with how to manage your time. Here are five of the best ways that you can dramatically increase your productivity.

TURN OFF ALL DISTRACTIONS

Every time an email pops up on your screen, every time your phone buzzes, or when your office door opens, your train of thought is destroyed. We all like to believe that we can both participate in a group chat and write our presentation, but the truth is, we canÕt. Your best work comes with silence. If you want to increase your productivity, then you have to turn off all the distractions.

STOP MULTITASKING

It can be incredibly tempting to want to try and take care of several tasks at once. However, it has been proven that multitasking just doesn't work. If you think that you can efficiently juggle phone calls, emails, and presentations without losing your productivity, you're fooling yourself. If you want to increase your productivity, you need to focus on one task at a time.

.

TAKE BREAKS

You might think that spending more time working will help you get more things done; however, when you're burned out, you will never work as well. Studies show that taking regular breaks during the day will dramatically help increase concentration and boost your mood. To help boost your productivity, take short breaks and walk around the office or grab a mid-day latte.

IMPLEMENT THE 2-MINUTE RULE

Make the most of your time by filling those tiny windows of downtime with actual tasks. Finding and completing tasks that take less than two minutes to finish will save you time during the day. If you have tasks that you can complete in two minutes or less, just jump in and do them.

TACKLE THE BIGGEST TASKS WHEN YOU ARE ALERT

Understanding when you work best is key to completing the big projects on time. No set schedule works for everyone. If you're a morning person, tackle your big tasks when you first start your day.

NOT EVERY DAY WILL BE PRODUCTIVE, SO DO NÕT BEAT YOURSELF UP OVER IT. INSTEAD, TRY TO REFOCUS YOUR ENERGY AND IMPLEMENT THESE PRODUCTIVITY TIPS INTO YOUR DAY. ONCE YOU FIND WHAT WORKS FOR YOU, YOUÕLL BE AMAZED AT HOW MUCH YOU CAN GET DONE.

SUBJECT: PLACES TO FIND LEADS FOR YOUR NETWORK MARKETING BUSINESS

PRL

Hey Entrepreneur ,

Did you know that there are actually many places to search for fresh leads besides cold calling or friend referrals?

Facebook is the largest online social networking website and boasts 500 millionusers. If you don't tap into Facebook you are literally shooting yourself in the foot.

Business forums are also great places to meet like minded individuals or people who are looking for networking opportunities.Just do a simple search and you'll find tons of such forums.

What about YouTube? Don't be suprised. YouTube has millions of searches for videos everyday and is owned by search engine giant - Google. This is definitely a place to find new leads if you know how to put together of good videos.

In short, don't limit yourself! There are tons of uncharted lands waiting to be conquered!

Talk soon,

Guidelines on how to peak affiliate programs to Promote

Everyone cannot have the same interests and passions.Likewise, not everyone will make an excellent affiliate. If you are promoting your product finding people who make good affiliates is crucial to success in internet marketing.This article will guide you on how to pick an affiliate program to promote.

People often place a great emphasis on quantity. While it is good to have a good number of affiliates, having quality rather than quantity is far more important and relevant. Three or four dedicated and experienced affiliates are more likely to make you more sales than 100 casual and inexperienced affiliates.Knowing the difference between the two will be the key to having a successful product.

One of the best ways to select your affiliates is to screen them. If you already have a list, you can send out emails looking for affiliates to promote your product. You can then screen interested applicants. Here are some questions you may like to ask.

What experience of affiliate marketing do you have? How do you intend to promote the product? What strategies do they intend to use? Do they have any personal interest in the product? If these criteria are met to your satisfaction, you will know that you have high-quality affiliates.

Once you have established that you have dedicated and enthusiastic affiliates on your books you need to give them the best chance of being successful. Train them. Give them all the steps and strategies needed to succeed.Give them copies of emails that they can send out to potential prospects.

Offering bonus prizes to your top affiliates creates healthy competition. Offering prizes can be a great motivation for affiliates to do well. Earning a reward is also synonymous with being appreciated for your efforts. Choose a prize that is relevant to the theme of the product that you are promoting. Try and think of prizes that are not too common. Having a prize that your affiliates will truly appreciate is a great incentive for them to do well.

Create a leaderboard. Similar to giving rewards, creating a leaderboard fosters healthy competition. Nobody wishes to come in last. Having a top ten or top 20 leaderboards is a great incentive for motivating affiliates. Everybody likes to be a winner, and you can tap into that winning mentality.

These are just several ways to pick and manage your affiliates. It is crucial that once you have selected good affiliates that you keep them motivated and show them how to promote your product.

Everyone needs to be encouraged. Implement some of these tips and you surely will be on your way to being a successful internet marketer.

PRL

DRESSING MISS

DAISY

LIVE FREE

PURA VIDA

FLOWER STYLES

WHO DOESN'T LOVE A FRESH PICKED FLORAL STACK?

ROBERT BALSLEY

THE LOSS OF INNOCENCE

From the battlements of Fort Extreme Irinushka Abramovich looked to the east through Dragon Pass. The fort is on the eastern edge of Draugen Pesta lands and the first line of defense against the Hyrokkin. Several miles away on the other side of the pass was the Hyrokkin fort which marked the beginning of their hereditary lands. A long-standing agreement between the two races marked the pass itself as neutral territory.

"I still don't see what you hope to accomplish, myshka," Fort Extreme's commandant, General Pavel Garin, said. He wore black, as did all Draugen Pesta's military forces. His silver-trimmed, black cape bellowed in the wind.

Irinushka looked over at the fort commander before returning her gaze back to the pass. "It could avert another war with the Hyrokkin, Pavel," she replied. "Maybe even put a truce in place that'll last more than a few weeks."

"Bah! We'll always be at war... at least until one of us figures out how to destroy the other."

Irinushka put a hand on Pavel's arm. "Don't say that. Both our peoples have a right to live in peace."

Pavel shook his head. "Irinushka, you're a priestess with a kind heart. But I think perhaps you have a naivety regarding the Hyrokkin that borders on insanity." Pavel took her hand. "They'll never honor a truce. They'll only use the time to get stronger and plot for our destruction. I've fought them. I know their butchering hearts. You don't."

"They honor the neutrality of the pass, Pavel. Maybe we can hope for something better?"

"I can give you a thousand reasons why those four-legged beasts honor the neutrality," Pavel replied hotly. His anger was growing by the minute because he knew she wouldn't listen... and that caused him to fear for her life. "But none of them have to do with honor!"

"It's the king's will," Irinushka said softly after a few moments of silence.

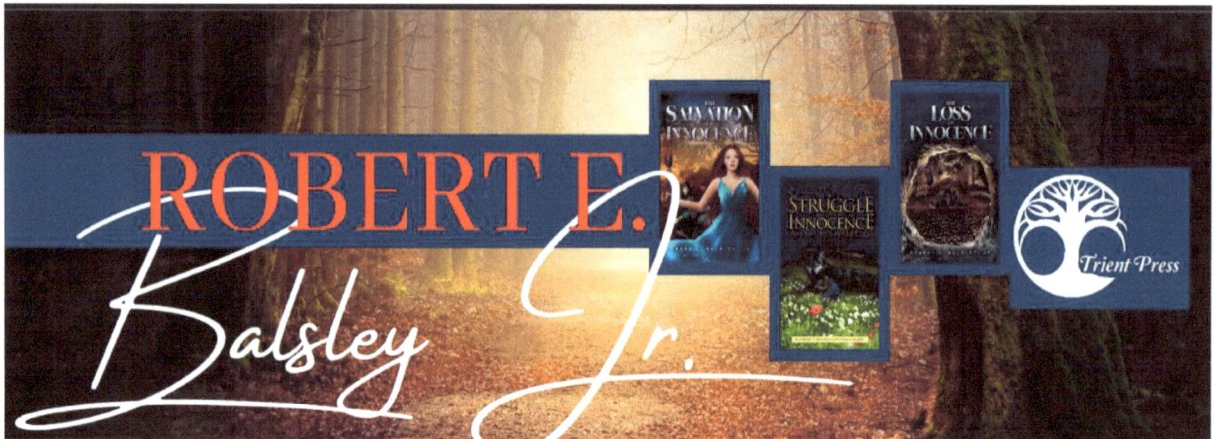

""Fedor was once a great warrior," Pavel replied. "Perhaps the finest our people had ever seen. But now he's old and weak... and not right in the head. He should have retired years ago. It still amazes me the people accept his leadership."

Irinushka sighed. She loved Pavel, but she was getting tired of constantly defending the king's position in this. "The people want peace," she said. "We've been at war with the Hyrokkin for centuries. Even warrior nations eventually tire of all the killing. Since they were the ones that asked for this meeting, maybe, just maybe, they feel the same. Lord Fedor simply wishes to explore the possibility."

Pavel brushed the side of Irinushka's face with the back of his hand. "Don't go, my love. If you're so certain about the Hyrokkin's intentions, then surely it can be handled by someone else. Send one of the king's lackeys."

"You know I can't do that," Irinushka replied as she wrapped her arm around his and laid her head on his shoulder.

"You're our High Priestess! As such you're far too valuable to our people... and to me personally... to be placed in such jeopardy."

Irinushka shook her head. "My position is irrelevant. I have my orders... as do you."
Pavel nodded. "My orders say nothing about how I'm to get you to the meeting... only that I do. I'm going with you. The High Priestess of the Draugen Pesta people should have a suitable escort."
"I was hoping you'd say that ," Irinushka said as she smiled. "Come. Tomorrow will be here soon. We need to rest... among other things."

FIND THE LOSS OF INNOCENCE HERE:
https://www.amazon.com/Loss-Innocence-Bridge-Magic-ebook/dp/B08R83RY2F/ref=sr_1_7?
dchild=1&keywords=robert+balsley&qid=1629746930&sr=8-7

BREAK THE SILENCE. BREAK THE CHAINS.

HELP STOP HUMAN TRAFFICKING

Join the fight at humantraffickinghotline.org

8 SECRET METHODS TO GROW YOUR PODCAST AUDIENCE

You spent a lot of time thinking about what gets talked about in your show. You want the best for your listeners. But, when you hit publish and check your stats a day later, you see only 10 people have listened to your latest episode. Sounds depressing, right? All that hard work with nothing to show for it. If you want your podcast to succeed, then you need to grow your podcast audience. Here's how:

1. Repurpose your podcast content

Podcasts may be in audio format, but the ball doesn't have to stop there. Turn your podcast content into blog posts, infographics, videos, social media graphics, and so much more!

2. Video yourself while recording your podcast

Let your followers see you live in action. They'll appreciate the sneak peek. Best of all, you can reach new audiences on YouTube and wherever else you upload your video.

3. Let your blog subscribers know about your podcast

Don't keep your blog subscribers in the dark. Rather, let them know you've got a new episode out and invite them to listen to it when they have time!

4. Post an update on your social media profiles

Everyone's on social media nowadays. Show people your social side and encourage them to listen to your podcast.

5. Interview experts in your niche

People love being recognized as experts. So, reach out to them and ask if they'd be willing to be interviewed. They'd be more than happy to promote your show to their followers, too!

6. Guest on more popular podcasts

If you position yourself as an 'expert' in your niche, you'll have people reaching out to you to interview you. Don't turn them down. Take the opportunity to prove your expertise and get people curious enough to follow your own show!

7. Advertise on social media

Organic social media traffic is possible, but it usually takes time. If you want to get the ball rolling, consider paying for ads. Facebook and Instagram are relatively cheap and you can easily target the right audience!

8. Create show notes or transcripts of each episode

Upload the show notes or transcripts to your blog, and make sure you optimize it for search engines. You just may see an avalanche of search engine traffic soon!

PRL

66 *4 Big Advantages of Blockchain*

At the heart of the excitement surrounding cryptocurrency is blockchain technology. Blockchain technology is the foundation that all virtual currencies are built upon. It is the decentralized and digital ledger technology that records all of the transactions without needed a financial intermediary, like a bank. Blockchain technology appears to offer four distinct advantages over existing payment facilitation networks.

Transparency

One of the main reasons why blockchain is so intriguing is that the technology is always open source. This means that other users and developers have the opportunity to change it as they see fit. Being open source makes altering logged data within the chain, complicated, making blockchain technology particularly secure.

Reduced Transaction Costs

Blockchain allows peer-to-peer and business-to-business transactions to be completed without having to work with a third-party. Without the involvement of a middleman, like a bank, tied to the transactions in a blockchain, the costs to the user or business can be significantly reduced over time.

Faster Transaction Settlements

When dealing with traditional banks, it isn't uncommon for a transaction to take days to become settled completely. This is because of the protocols established in bank transferring software, as well as the fact that most financial institutions are only open during the day. Blockchain technology, on the other hand, works 24 hours a day, seven days a week, which means transactions made with the blockchain technology can be processed more quickly.

Decentralization

Another reason why blockchain technology is so exciting is its lack of a central data hub. Rather than having to run a massive data center and verifying the transactions through the center, blockchain technology allows individual transactions to have their own proof of validity, as well as the authorization to enforce the constraints. Since information on a particular blockchain is piecemealed on individual servers throughout the world, it ensures that if hackers stole the data, they would only gain a small amount of data and not the entire network, keeping it from becoming completely compromised.

Even with these advantages, there is still a significant worry that can't be overlooked. Throughout history, investors have continued to overestimate how quickly a new technology will be adopted. Like most new technologies it will take time to lay the groundwork for blockchain, and it could still be some years before businesses fully embrace this technology as a significant component of their payment systems.

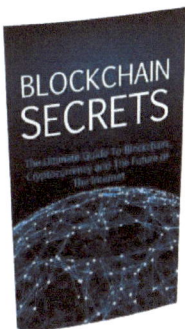

For more about blockchain
please visit https://trientpressmagazine.com/

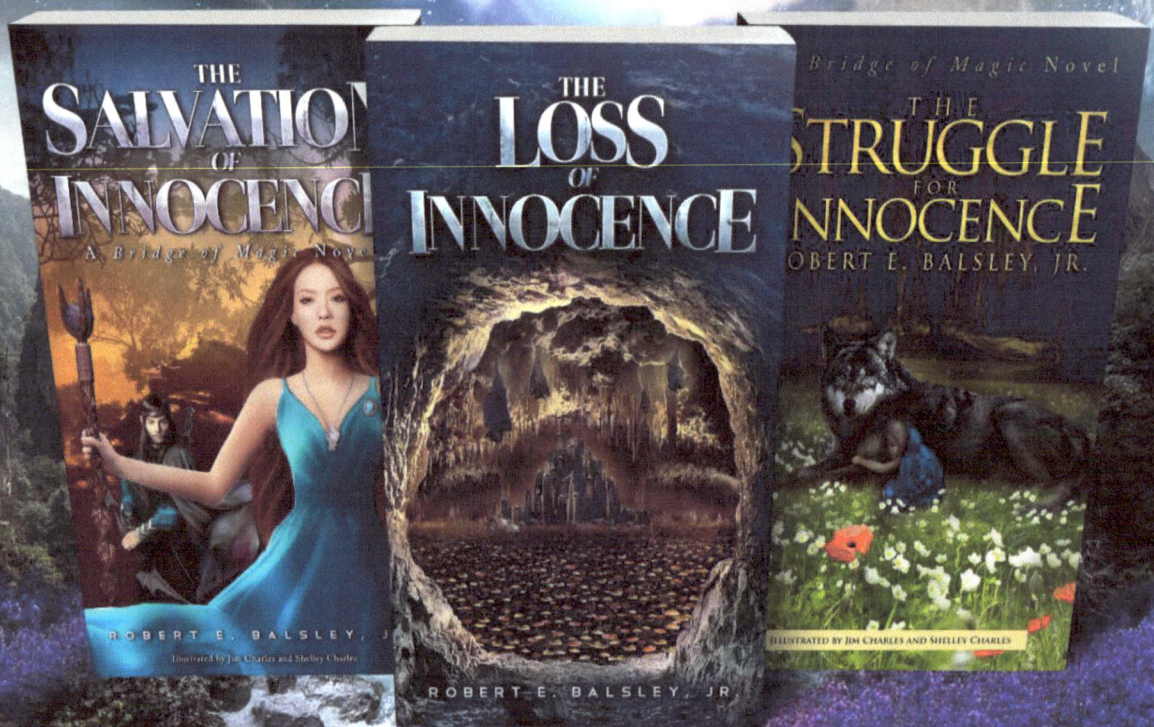

Author Spotlight

ROBERT BALSLEY

THE ROBERT BALSLEY COLLECTION

A BRIDGE OF MAGIC

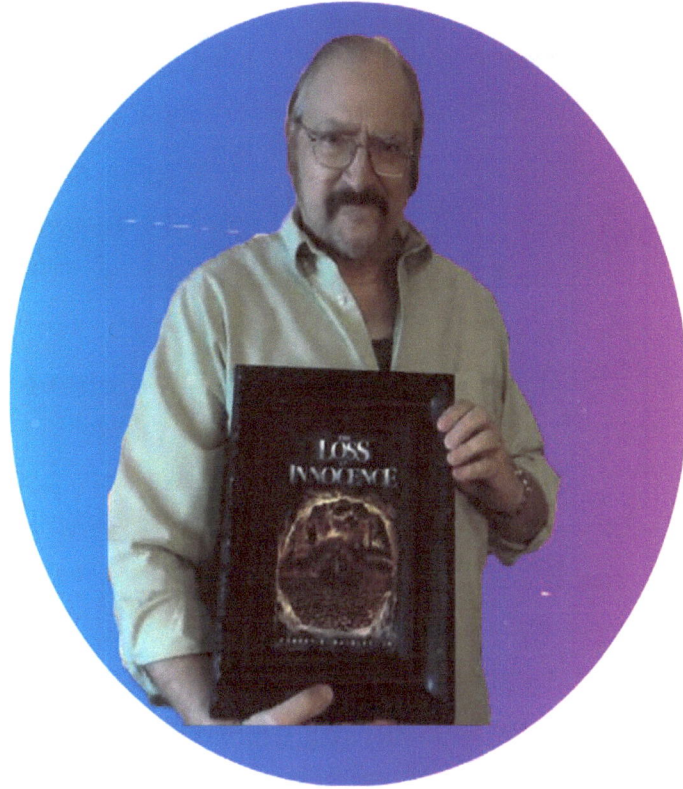

Author Spotlight

ROBERT BALSLEY

Robert Balsley here. I never suspected I wanted to be a writer, but then I was introduced to Dungeon and Dragons, where everything changed. I can't get ideas out of my head... so I write books to soothe my passion.

ABOUT ROBERT E. BALSLEY

"The magnificently incredible brought to life."
Robert E. Balsley, Jr. (1954 -) was born in Sioux City, Iowa. At the age of four his parents moved their family to Cincinnati, Ohio. Upon graduation from high school in 1973, Robert joined the United States Air Force which sent him to Tinker Air Force Base, Oklahoma. Upon his discharge in 1979, he found employment as a civil servant on Tinker until his retirement in 2014. In 2018 Robert and his wife picked up roots and moved from Oklahoma to Burlington, Kentucky, which is just across the Ohio River from Cincinnati.

In 1990 he played his first game of Dungeons and Dragons and was soon writing his own games. From this sprang the ideas which ultimately led to his love of writing and the creation of his current novels. Many of the main characters are based upon actual people who played Dungeons and Dragons with him all those years. This includes personalities, idiosyncrasies, and all those other traits that make friends so endearing... and fictional characters so alive!

Throughout his life he's been an avid reader of science fiction and fantasy. Isaac Asimov, James Bliss, David Eddings, George R.R. Martin, Terry Goodkind, and Robert Heinlein are among his favorite authors. Robert's also a collector of figures and models such as Star Trek spaceships, WWII airplanes, Dungeons and Dragons miniatures, TV and movie monster figures (particularly Godzilla), and dragons to name a few. It's in this world of mankind's rich imagination that he develops his stories, plots, subplots, heroic and cowardly deeds, laughter, tears (and all the emotions in between) that make tales come alive for the reader... that makes the reader want to "turn the page".

THE SALVATION OF INNOCENCE

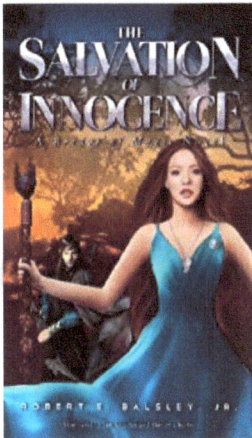

A young woman embarks on a harrowing journey to save her world's last vestige of magical healing in Robert E. Balsley Jr.'s epic new fantasy novel, The Salvation of Innocence.

Althaya, the goddess of healing, wishes to share her ability to help those in need, providing "empaths," which give clerics the means to magically heal others-a means that some people fear and wish to destroy. In response, a dark magic known as the Purge is created to seek out and eradicate all empaths.

But one lone survivor remains, spirited away by Althaya and hidden in a magical stasis field. There, the last empath must remain alive until the time comes for rescue-but the Purge will not rest until the last empath is found and killed.

Three thousand years later, Kristen Rosilie Clearwater is only beginning to realize her destiny. Having been brought to the island of InnisRos as an orphan, she has long felt a "tug" toward something she can't quite understand. But when she begins experiencing the dreams of a young child, Kristen knows that the two are somehow connected-and that the fate of the world, and the future of healing magic, rests on.

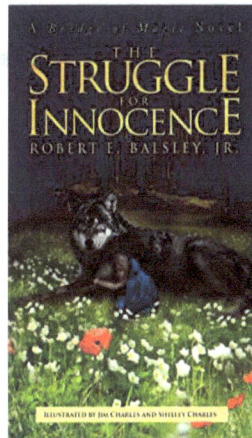

THE STRUGGLE FOR INNOCENCE

In this suspenseful sequel to The Salvation of Innocence, the war against evil rages on. This time good must fight on two fronts to stop a great evil-one strong enough to commit genocide-or their world will be changed forever.

After barely escaping death at the hands of the vampire Lukas, Emmy still faces an even greater threat. The Purge is approaching. Emmy and her comrades' only chance is to get help from the sentient city of Elanesse and commit the first assault.

Far way, another conflict is brewing. Father Horatio Goram must face off against the power-hungry First Counselor Mordecai Lannian, whose demonic concubine pushes for war, but the odds are against him. Emmy's fate rests on this struggle, and this determined priest will do anything to win.

In a realm where healing magic relies on a single emissary's ability to commune with the gods, Emmy's death would have wide repercussions. This sensational thriller reveals the destructive power evil will use to achieve its dastardly ends-and the depths to which good must go to stop it.

The third book in this compelling series, The Loss of Innocence, is upcoming

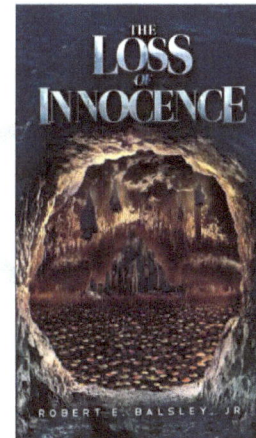

THE LOSS OF INNOCENCE

War has come to InnisRos!

The Ak-Séregon Stone, stolen by the demon Nightshade, has been used to force open a corridor between Aster and the Svartalfheim, the home world of the Dark Elves. The Dark Elf army, led by Nightshade's father, Aikanáro, marches on InnisRos. Only Father Goram and his allies, with Queen Lessien's army, can close down the corridor and break the stranglehold the Dark Elves have on the island of the Elves of Light.

But the Dark Elf invasion of InnisRos is only one phase of Nightshade's design. To ensure InnisRos' human allies stay on their side of the world, she blackmails Lord Ternborg, leader of the Draugen Pesta, the Black Death, to invade the mainland from the east. Forced to collaborate with the mercenary cities of HeBron and Madeira, Lord Ternborg reluctantly leads three armies into the Forest of the Fey and the surrounding valley to capture the sorcerer stronghold of Havendale. Tangus, Kristen, Emmy and the humans now have their own war to fight on the mainland.

Meanwhile, deep below the surface, a new threat arises. The sylph are awake and moving from the depths with one goal in mind... destroy all life on Aster.

Victorious PR

🌐 https://victoriouspr.com/

✉️ support@victoriouspr.com

📞 (702) 718- 5821

We are Victorious PR

Victorious PR is an award-winning firm that helps Entrepreneurs and Businesses get featured in industry-specific media, local press, podcasts, and top publications to be seen as Industry Leaders in their fields. Victorious PR has worked with major brokerages such as JPAR and multi-millionaire entrepreneurs such as Dan Henry and Krista Mashore to build their authority and credibility in the press. We have secured placements on such places as Forbes, Entrepreneur, Business Insider, Inman, National Mortgage News, PBS, TV & radio stations, Facebook and Instagram verification, and the TEDx stage.

Don't take our word for it

"I swear GOLD. If your clients don't know you, they aren't being put with you and Victoria has helped me overcome that and so much more. She got me on about Farrah and it. It absolutely blew my mind. I've been over the moon with the quality of work."

Bao Le | CEO of Bao Digital

Praise from the
Real Estate Industry

"Victoria did an amazing thing. She moved through that. I never even thought of reaching to different publications and getting us seen to those publications with stories and was able to get us sent to the PR and which in a huge local newspaper. And I got a lot of personal private messages. She uncovered a lot of ways to get in front of and my face out in front of people that I would have never imagined. I loved how I been in front of."

Coltyn Simmons Founder of Custom Fit Real Estate

Praise from the
Entrepreneurs Industry

"I have to say a great job, Victoria "Thank you so much. As the work has were wonderful and I love having the guys behind my name now. I just gave to more credibility."

Krista Mashore Coach, Best Selling Author

FEATURED IN:

inman Forbes Entrepreneur yahoo! finance

abc TODAY GSD FOX NEWS

📷 thevictoriakennedy f @thevictoriouspr 🐦 @GoVictoriaK in victoriajkennedy

What We Do

We create Industry Leaders
We help businesses be seen as the #1 Authority in their niche.

Your next giant leap leans on more than metrics, channels, and platforms alone. It requires a pitch-perfect mix of strategic precision, deeply human thinking, creative prowess, and some love.

Victorious PR is a global agency working across fields to build brands that attract, brands that offer a unique position, and brands that effect real change in the world.

REAL ESTATE	ENTREPRENEURS	AND SO MUCH MORE...
Although the real estate mantra is "location, location, location," we're all about "public relations, public relations, public relations." What good is a great loaction's availability if no one knows about it?	No matter what stage of business you're in, know that your story matters. We put you in the forefrount to get the right notoeriety you deserve.	

One Of Our Success Stories

While most people can't handle one job, Farrah Ali has three. During the day she is a fulltime insurance professional, at night she is a full time investor and she is the author of Diaries of a Female Real Estate Investor. To top it all off, the most important job for her is being a single mother to her two kids.

Farrah has been a crucial piece to the growth of Chicago REIA since the beginning. Her journey with investing started in June of 2014, now just four short years later she is at twenty-five rental properties, one flip, and eight wholesale deals.

FARRAH ALI

Real Estate Investor, Entrepreneur & Author

www.farrahali.org

DIARIES OF A FEMALE REAL ESTATE INVESTOR

Learn How A Single Mom Went From 80k In Debt To A Multi Million Dollar Portfolio

FARRAH ALI

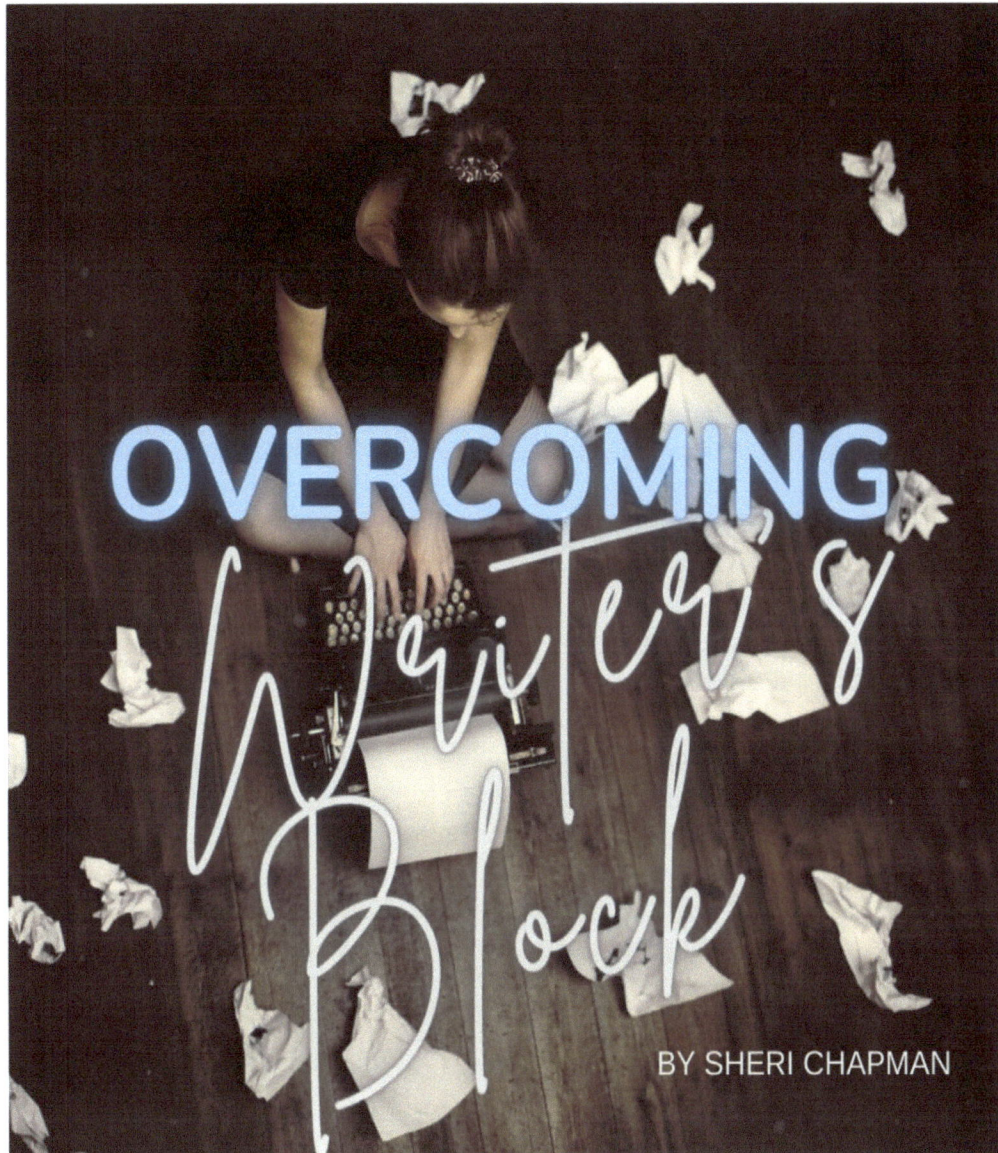

OVERCOMING Writer's Block

BY SHERI CHAPMAN

What is writer's block? Most writers know without explanation. It is a time when you simply cannot proceed in your story or article. You are stumped with where to go or how to move the plot forward.

As an author, I went many years without having experienced this. My first real experience was with my second story, *Passions of the Heart*. I literally put it down for years. The danger in this tactic is: will you ever pick it up again? Luckily, I did.

So, what causes writer's block? Basically, you are not able to access your creative force due to some discontent.

Here are some tips. Some I use, and some I should.

1. Develop a writing routine
Habits come with practice. Figure out a schedule for writing that works for you. Is it a set time per day, every other day, or once a week? Set a goal for writing and keep to it. Your environment for writing helps. Have that special nook reserved. Your brain will recognize what to do when you sit down there (with practice).

2. Don't get stumped by formalized writing – the mechanics of writing
I think many people are perfectionists, and we would like our drafts to need little editing. However, this can be a great block to creative flow. Don't worry about word use, repetitive phrases, punctuation, or grammar. This is a draft. Whipping it into shape can come later.

3. Visit other forms of creativity
Look at other peoples' work. Read a book, even revisit a favorite from your past. Watch a movie. Visit an art gallery. Paint some pottery. Even walking in nature can reset our creative flow.

4. Free write through it
 This can be a separate document, but just write down your thoughts continuously without pause. The subject can be on the piece you're working on, random thoughts, or it can be something completely different. The process of writing will help remove that stone or boulder you're working around. Until you get used to doing this, set a time limit (ten minutes?) where you force yourself to push through it.
 Also, don't intend to write for a purpose. Sometimes if we are writing a story for someone or for a market, it can block our flow. Just write. Worry about formalities later.

5. Stay focused
 Turn off that television, music, and internet.

6. Mix up the order of your piece
Sometimes starting at the beginning of your story can be hard. You know where you want to go but aren't sure of how to get there. Start where your mind is and work from there. The beginning will come. You can work backwards or use flashbacks. Just write!

7. Do something that doesn't require thought
Do something that's automatic. When I'm driving or walking, my mind often wanders. I often think about my stories, even when I'm trying to listen to an audible book (and find myself rewinding multiple times). Even a bath or such can bring a moment of enlightenment.

8. Change it up – do something different
a. Change your point of view by writing a section through another character's eyes. You don't have to publish this part, but it can help restore the flow.
b. Take a break and look at writing prompts. You can find them on the internet or social media. I subscribe to them. Many of my stories have come from anthology calls.

9. Work on your characters
a. Make them full characters – three dimensional – with flaws, strengths, and personality. Do they have goals? What are their fears?
b. Motivations – what motivates your character(s) – explain why they are necessary in your story
c. Character history and development – what do they look like? What do they believe? Where did they come from (past history)? Explain mannerisms, emotions, etc.

10. Reread.
 When it's been a while, especially, reread your story. It will help you remember and get excited about it again.

Fear or self-doubt.
Who doesn't experience this? Not only with writing, but with life? Push it away and write anyway. Prove yourself wrong or work through it by doing the opposite of what fear is telling you to do (Run away, you can't do this.).

Harsh self-judgment/criticism.
Stop beating yourself up and just write. Most of the time, individuals are his/her own worst critic. That is until you work with your editor (Ha ha!)

Comparing oneself to others.

It's a common thing to do, especially if you live in the United States where everything is a competition. However, compete against yourself. You really can't compare apples to oranges equally.

Unrealistic expectations.
When I first attempted to get published, I wanted in a "big" house. While those fortunate examples do exist, most of us have to start off with baby steps and work our way up. That doesn't mean we aren't successful.

A block to your flow.
What is going on in your real life? Most of us aren't problem-free. Bigger problems, however, do block our flow. Are there issues with the job? Family? Money? You have to learn how to repress your worries to write. My answer is meditation and manifesting thought. It truly does work for me if I make time for this practice.

Sheri Chapman loves life and laughing, but you couldn't tell it by her work - from historical romances, suspense, dark fiction, or horror stories. A former teacher of thirty years and mother to four grown daughters, you can follow her on Facebook, Instagram and Twitter to find links to her books.

PODCASTING
PROFIT SECRETS

Trient Press

BUILDING YOUR BRAND

PODCAST MARKETING

PODCASTING PROFIT SECRETS

PODCAST MARKETING

LEARN HOW YOU CAN LAUNCH YOUR PODCAST
QUICKLY, EASILY & AFFORDABLY!

Need more profits in your pocket?

www.trientpressmagazine.com

M.I. Ruscsak

The Art of Podcasting

Today, it seems that everyone has a podcast. From our International music professionals, actors, actresses, and entertainers in general to our children and parents, all one must do is share the special recipe on how to make a favorite dish. It truly seems like everyone has a podcast.

Twenty years ago, we didn't foresee places like YouTube becoming an international sensation by bringing us information from motivational speeches to how to cook pasta. For those that created spaces like YouTube, I'm sure they saw the potential, but today, in a flooded market, how do you get your podcast, your station, your Channel, your message to stand out? This can seem like a daunting task, but there is a science behind this.

If you follow Trient Press Magazine online, you might have come across one of our many tools to help you succeed. One example is The Big Book Network Marketing A-Z. or Podcast Marketing. You might even have been curious enough to go ahead and purchase one or both books. However, if you're still on the fence about purchasing a book, that's okay. I'm still here to help.

What makes a successful podcast? As a podcaster myself, I can tell you it takes a lot of hard work, and you will not become an overnight success. For every one person that has 100,000 followers or more, there are hours of hard work that you do not see. There can be even years. It's about creating content that is true to you but also will appeal to the masses.

Entertainers have this sort of cornered. We already know their names, we know their faces, and for die-hard fans we will follow them no matter what. However, for the new podcaster, it is a little bit more difficult. We have to learn how to hashtag. Many don't even know what a hashtag is. A hashtag is that symbol that used to be called the pound symbol or be an abbreviation for the word, "number". Most have seen this used from Facebook to Twitter to Instagram. But what do they really do?

Dean Rotbart
Pulitzer Prize-winning
Dove and Dragon

No matter what site you're on, if you see a hashtag, the words following the symbol are being tracked. Every time it shows up in social media, it raises the rank of whatever the symbol is posted to. In the case of podcasting, if you use #dovenddragonradio and put it into any search engine, you will find all the podcast posts across all social media. Now if you look for just the dove and dragon radio via YouTube, it will bring you to that site. If a podcaster is using other hashtags, not just your station, they might use multiple hashtags. For example, say the podcaster had a great interview with Pulitzer Prize-winning Journalist Dean Rotbart, he/she might use a hashtag just for #DeanRotbart or #PulitzerPrize-winning. Using hashtags is the first step in gaining your audience.

The true work comes with the podcast itself. You have to be authentic. You have to be personable. If you go back to the Dove and dragon radio podcast from the very beginning, you will see a different me. You can actually hear the difference in my voice. Did I change as an individual? Not really. Did my axle voice change? No, I don't think it has. However, I have changed as an individual. I have changed from being that scared in my show. I really didn't know what I was doing. Yet, this is my show, these are my interviews, and I'm here to get my clients' messages out. I know my own program. No, I do not mean I actually own the station, but rather, I take ownership of what happens on the program.

I have changed my mindset from I don't know what I'm doing to I'm going to do it and I'm going to have fun. Every podcast is authentic, and I love to talk about anything and the message behind it. Depending on the guests, that message changes. I could be interviewing about this great book that is just getting ready to come out or doing an interview with a multimillion-dollar CEO talking about how they want to help individuals get themselves out of poverty. I could be talking to someone who is an independent that doesn't agree with the government on either end of the spectrum and wants to yell at the top of their lungs to make people understand this. It's not so much about what I do, but what their message is.

❝❝*I Changed my mindset...*❞

Do I, as a podcaster, agree with every person that comes on my station? No, there's no way any one person can agree with everyone all the time. However, instead of causing controversy and turning the show into a yelling match, I take a different route, and it seems to be working. I do not want to argue with you but I do want to have a casual conversation with you. If you argue with someone, your message gets lost and never in my podcast do I want the message to get lost. I want people to hear the entire message.

For best success, there is an art to podcasting: your successful podcasters have spent hours upon hours honing their craft. For myself, I have spent the last three years honing my channel to accommodate the type of messages that I want for my listeners. It's really up to you about what you want on your channel and how you want to go about doing it, but you have to understand the science behind it. It boils down to this: how you brand your product.

If you argue with someone your message gets lost

The purpose of the podcasts is getting the message out there. The message could pertain to cooking, how to play a game, or any other reason. You have to get your message out there. However, if you're causing controversy, just to cause controversy, then what is your message? However, if you're causing a ripple of discord in a respectful fashion where you're interested in having a true conversation that we all need to have, then your message will be better received.

GET YOUR YOUNG HUSTLERS CONFERENCE SEAT!

The Young Hustler Conference Was Created For MOTIVATED PEOPLE To Reach Their GOALS By Bringing In Some Of The Top Experts In Business, Marketing, Sales, Scaling, Money And Finance.

MEET THE SPEAKERS

Matt Buchanan is the founder of Pioneers of Marketing and the Young Hustler Conference.

Matt has been featured on Forbes #1 Marketing Conference the 10X Growth Con sharing the stage with Magic Johnson, Floyd Mayweather, Grant Cardone, Usher, John Travolta and others because of how fast his business has grown. Matt's helped to get almost everyone on Grant Cardone's executive team the Instagram Blue Check and has worked as a social media director for a fortune 5000 fastest growing company.

Matt took his business from $60k a year to over $3.5 million in annual revenue in less than 13 months, going from $20k in debt to storing over $1,000,000 in cash in less than a year and going from working in his child bedroom to opening a beautiful office in Houston and now Miami, all at 23 years old with zero outside capital and zero investors. This year he's now on pace to do $10 million in revenue but what he's most proud of his helping people on his team such as Giovanni make over $10,000 his first month joining the team!

His goal is now to create a $150 million dollar company, help 10,000 small business owners reach their goals and create an army of 500 young hustlers and help them reach their goals and have fun while doing so. His passion is helping other people achieve business success. For years Matt struggled to find the right strategies to win in business and his goal is to use the Young Hustler Conference to spread this message to others who are going through those same struggles while creating a network of like minded people.

Act Now

SEATS ARE LIMITED

American boxer Floyd Mayweather was born on February 24, 1977, in Grand Rapids, Michigan.

Floyd is known as the best defensive boxer in **history** and is undefeated at 50-0. He topped the Forbes and Sports Illustrated lists of the 50 highest-paid athletes of 2012 and 2013, and the Forbes list again in both 2014 and 2015, listing him as the highest-paid athlete in the world. In 2018, Mayweather was the most-paid athlete in the world, with earnings amounting to $275 million. He's a champion at the highest level!

Brandon Dawson founded his first company at age 28, Sonus, where he served as Founder and CEO for seven years. He learned a lot about raising money from high net worth individuals, private equity firms and strategic partnerships. Over five years, he made over 150 presentations to raise capital, completed over 100 acquisitions, and created distribution agreements with over one thousand independent business owners and dozens of suppliers. With four separate equity raises totaling 38 million dollars, and negotiating 20 million in strategic debt financing he learned a lot about the process, and different equity and debt structures, not to mention negotiation skills in purchasing businesses.

He's now direct business partners with Discovery TV Show Star Grant Cardone. Brandon sold his last business for **$151 million dollars** and is now helping others scale their business. He's personally made me millions of dollars and he made this great training below on the top elements needed to scale your business.

November 5 & 6

Florida International University

https://www.younghustlerconference.com/

The Nature of Fear

BY SHERI CHAPMAN

Fear. Is it a good thing or is it bad? One cannot truly rule one way or another. For millennial, fear has been the primary thing that kept us alive. Even in the animal kingdom, those wild species must rely on fear to keep them safe. After all, natural selection ensures only the strongest survive.

The world we are living in today is a very scary place. From invasions by terrorists – ahem – the Taliban in Kabul, Afghanistan, to climate change accelerated by wildfires in the tundra, the very nature of what we fear has grown and twisted. Stock market drops, a deadly, man-created virus that mutates on a whim, freedom of choice taken away, and the list goes on. The question is: what can we do?

We are truly living in a Stephen King novel. Every time we think we have solutions, it seems the response to our efforts only worsens. It appears that we are helpless. So, how do we respond? Run, hide, fight is what we are taught and is what has worked for years. They are our only known responses to fear. Many want to give up and hide. Running does no good. So, we must continue to fight. We must continue to study the things we fear to combat a response.

Many Christians must be wondering, Has Armageddon arrived? If you believe this, then a big answer would be prayer. If you are more of a spiritual being, is the answer any different? I believe not. Call prayer whatever term you like, but the world needs to unite and send forth healing vibrations.

I am not only praying and meditating on world peace, the ozone to mend, for the women in Afghanistan (and all citizens), but for the Earth itself. She will continue to exist, but will we without a healthy land to stand on with stable air quality?

Man has created all the issues we see. We do not have time for science to reverse the effects of what we have created. Can the Ozone even be repaired? I do not know. But I do know I've seen many miracles occur in my lifetime through prayer and meditation or by manifesting thought. Please join me by sending out healing vibrations to the world and all who are in it.

Sheri Chapman loves life and laughing, but you couldn't tell it by her work - from historical romances, suspense, dark fiction, or horror stories. A former teacher of thirty years and mother to four grown daughters, you can follow her on Facebook, Instagram and Twitter to find links to her books.

Blessings,

SHERI CHAPMAN

ADVICE

Well Being

BY: HOLLY K BROOKS
INTUITIVE LIFE COACH & PSYCHIC READER IN THE UNITED STATES
ONE-ON-ONE READINGS & SPIRITUAL LIFE COACHING
IF YOU ARE WRESTLING WITH A CHALLENGE THAT NEEDS AN ANSWER, PLEASE SEND
YOUR QUESTIONS TO TRIENT PRESS MAGAZINE.....

ADVICE

Hello Holly K,

I love my husband. My mother-in-law, not so much. She is toxic to my marriage. Her constant interfering, meddling, correcting me in front of my children. Hellish! I have been married for eleven years. In the name of peace, I really try to get along with her. Now, I have reached my emotional limit where she is concerned. You would think that my children's Nana would love to babysit or come over to visit. A hard pass. If she babysits all she does is read the paper, drink coffee and yell at my children.
I am at my wit's end, she is nasty to me, as well as just stopping by whenever she feels like it. Please tell me how to handle this, without kidnapping or having her knees broken (nervous jokes).

Signed,
Did I really marry his mother as well?

Dear mess of his mother,

This is personal for you, yet very common. It is time to have a serious sit down with your hubby. How he handles his mother is paramount. He needs to see and understand what dear old mom is doing. Give him all the facts. Let him read this letter, that should do it. With his support you both can lay out some "Mother-in-law" boundaries. These boundaries must be enforced, so she knows you mean business.
I know this new Mother-in-law map will begin to ease the tension she creates. Let me know how it goes.

Family Dynamics,

Holly K

ADVICE

Dear Holly K,

I am mom to 3 daughters. They are 4, 7 and 10. They are good kids and quite a challenge. My 10-year-old is entering that "tween" age (and all of the loveliness that comes with it. LOL). All
her friends have cell phones. She is very independent. No longer am I needed to make her playdates. She handles her comings and goings. Last week she was gone for 24 hours, between different houses, swimming, and a sleepover. If she had a cell phone, she would be able to call or text me. She is very good about letting me know (she has her dad's old flip phone). The fly in the ointment is, he is receiving her texts & face time calls on his cell while he is working. He is not happy. There were no cell phones when I was her age. I want to make sure that she isn't too young. I will have appropriate apps. Like "365" and "Barker". This will allow me to see everything she does on her phone, as well as her location. I own the phone when she is home. Please advise!

Signed,
Confused Cyber Mom

Dear Cyber Mom,

Your old Holly K is thrilled about the lack of social media, cell phones and the Internet when my daughter was growing up. Mom's today have so much more to deal with due to technology. I don't envy you. On social media girls that are 10, dress and act like they are 14. OH Mylanta! For practical reasons, like staying in touch, knowing where she is and getting her interference off your husband's phone while he is doing business- a big YES. As usual boundaries must be enforced. One false move, you just take her phone away. She will throw a fit, tell you she hates you and that you are not the boss of her. You are!!! When you deem it so, give her back her precious phone and try again. You mentioned 2 other daughters. Get your cyber feet wet with your eldest; then you will know how to handle her sisters when they are 10. Don't over think this. Go for it!

Signed,
What do we do with all of this technology?

Holly K

ADVICE

Hi Holly K,

Well, I never thought this would be on my radar, but it is! I have an 8-year-old son. For the last three years he has been telling me that he is a girl. When this first started, he was 5. Easy to talk about this, I let him play with dolls instead of trucks. At 6 he wanted to wear my lipstick. I was somewhat thrown off my game, however I let him, sometimes when he was in the house. Now he is 8 and is dressing a lot more like a girl. I am concerned of what he will be facing from his peers, other adults, and teachers.

I have read many books on the subject. This situation is who he feels he is. Knowing what he/she is walking into in his life, should I encourage this or discourage the subject entirely? HELP.

Signed,
He or She?

Dear Major Mommy,

Today's world is opening to various gender fluidity, kids wanting to be called she (as in your case). Your son did not just make this up. He let you know when he was 5, yet I am sure he knew this earlier. These situations should be handled with knowledge and loving care. For you to discourage him and ignore the subject, will only serve to backfire for both of you. You must not make him feel that this is forbidden or bad. It will eat away at his confidence and self-esteem. All the while confusing you both and create an atmosphere of tension and instability. Read everything you can. Handle this with care, as he/she is your cherished child. Speak with his guidance counselor, as well with his teachers. The world is unstable as it is, giving him support will help him to figure this out without fear of retribution.

This is new and you will rise to the occasion. There is nothing wrong with his feelings.

Signed,

Holly K

Influencers

Every Entrepreneur Know these sites

Upfluence - Find Influencers
https://get.upfluence.com/

Find & Recruit Influencers - GRIN - Influencer Marketing
https://grin.co/

AspireIQ (formerly Revfluence)
https://www.aspireiq.com/

HypeAuditor - Top Instagram Influencers Ranking
https://hypeauditor.com/

Post for Rent
https://www.postforrent.com/

Dovetale
https://dovetale.com/

Influence.co
https://Influence.co

collabstr
https://collabstr.com/

socialseo
https://www.socialseo.com/

sproutsocial
https://sproutsocial.com/

Heepsy | Find influencers worldwide
https://www.heepsy.com/

awario
https://awario.com/

Klear
https://klear.com/

Traackr
https://www.traackr.com/

Afluencer
https://afluencer.com/

RESOURCES FOR PODCASTING

Courses

How to Start a Podcast - Podcasting Made Easy

https://www.udemy.com/powerpodcasters

Scott Paton's 9-hour podcasting course is one of the highest rated courses on Udemy. This course is great for anyone who wants to know
how to make a podcast and it covers practically everything there is to know about this medium! And yes, according to reviews, this show is
great even for absolute beginners.

Podcasting Success Strategies: Get Podcast Sponsorships

https://www.udemy.com/podcast-sponsorships

One of the top 'mysteries' of podcasting is how to make money from it. Well, sponsorships are one of the most popular money-making techniques in the podcast world, but it's not easy to get into. Finding, approaching and pitching to potential sponsors isn't exactly easy. If this is something you're very interested in, then you should sign up for this course!

Professional Podcast Production, Editing & Blueprint

https://www.udemy.com/professional-podcast-production

One of the most difficult aspects of podcasting is the technical side of things. The level of your technical skills will greatly affect the quality of
your show, hence it's important to be well versed with the technical side. Ian Robinson's course is the bestselling course on Udemy on this topic.
He'll teach you everything there is to know about recording, editing, uploading and publishing your podcast!

How I Got 50+ Podcast Appearances Using RadioGuestList

https://www.udemy.com/how-i-got-50-podcast-appearances-using-radioguestlist

Getting interviewed on other, more popular podcasts is a great way to get the word out about your show. You'll also establish your authority
and your status as an 'expert' in your niche. In this course, you'll learn how you can do this on your own without spending thousands of dollars
on a publicist!

Blogs and Websites

Entrepreneurs On Fire

https://www.eofire.com

John Lee Dumas is the man behind the ultra-popular Entrepreneurs on
Fire podcast. He's interviewed over 2,000 guests on the show and covers everything there is to know about podcasting, marketing, and entrepreneurship in general. You can listen to all 2,000+ episodes directly from his blog. He earns six figures every month with a huge Chunk coming from his show's sponsors.

The Audacity To Podcast

https://theaudacitytopodcast.com

Daniel J. Lewis has published over 300+ episodes on this show. He talks about the ins and outs of podcasting, the software Audacity, and blogging on WordPress. While the podcast hasn't been updated in a while (he cited personal issues), his show is literally still a goldmine for podcasters of all levels. Check the 'Get Started' section first for a list of recommended episodes and resources.

The Libsyn Blog

http://blog.libsyn.com

Libsyn is one of the most popular podcasthosts around, so it's not surprising that they publish a lot of valuable content on their blog. Their blog categories include promoting and marketing your podcast, hosting, Libsyn updates, podcasting news/events/tips/gear, and more. Plus, they even interview Libsyn podcasters, so if you're planning to host on Libsyn, there's a chance you could get interviewed on their blog!

Smart Passive Income's Podcasting Blog
https://www.smartpassiveincome.com/podcasting
Pat Flynn is a well-known digital marketing expert, having been hands⊠
on with his online businesses for well over a decade now. His blog has a
solid section on podcasting. He offers free courses and tutorials on
podcasting. He's also neatly categorized his podcasting page with links
to his top content on podcasting (tips, interviews, content workflow, case
studies, and more)

Ground Zero On 9/11 with
THE WALL STREET JOURNAL

September Twelfth

An American
Comeback Story

By: Dean Rotbart

SEPTEMBER TWELFTH

An American Comeback Story

As Seen On...

FOX NEWS

abc

CBS NEWS

NBC

TRIENT PRESS

Magazine

Trientrepreneur

A Trient Press Publication for Authors & Entrepreneurs

Issue 5 | August 2021
$10.99

FEATURED

Seed Money: Black
Entrepreneurs Hope
Pandemic Gardening Boom
Will Grow Healthier Eating

ARTICLES

Four Time Management
Tactics for Busy
Entrepreneurs

Understanding the
Law of Attraction

TIPS

Must have information
for both authors and
entrepreneurs

GUEST ARTICLES

Have something to share with
Authors and Entrepreneurs
submit a story to:
info@trientmagaize.com

INTERVIEWS

For radio interviews there is a fee:
https://calendly.com/mlruscsak-
ceo/30min

For free printed interviews Contact Info@trientpress.com